I AM AN AMERICAN

(The Poem)

Written & Designed by:

Vivian L. Childs

V.L. Childs
Publishing

CEO: Minister Vivian L. Childs
CFO: Colonel Henry Childs (Ret)
COO: Henry Childs II
D. O: Ashante Y. Everett
D. M Nakeisha M. Curry M.D.

V.L. Childs Publishing
V.L.CHILDS/UICF LLC
P.O. Box 9334
Warner Robins, GA 31095
vlccreations@yahoo.com
www.vivianlchilds.com

First published by V.L. Childs 3/6/2017
ISBN: 978-0-9799896-5-0

Author: Vivian L. Childs

Editorial Team: Henry Childs, Nakeisha M. Curry, Mack W. Curry III, Ashante Y. Everett, Judy Dienst

Cover/Layout design: Vivian L. Childs

This book is given to:

____

I AM AN AMERICAN~

On this ____day of ________________

In the year of ________________

From: __________________________

Occasion: ____________________

Dedication Page

This book is dedicated to those I love, respect, honor, and cherish.

I owe thanks to my heavenly Father, who watches over me daily, who favors me, and who is my Shield of Faith. Without Him, none of this matters. He blessed me to have the best parents imaginable. They instilled, they nurtured, and they loved. More importantly, because of their union, I exist.

To my husband, my children, and my grandchildren, we are one. We are not perfect, we make mistakes, but having each other means we are never alone. Our undeniable love is real and unconditional. Thank you for loving me.

Lastly, I have been fortunate to live aboard and believe me, I am proud be an American.

Author

Vivian L. Childs

Executive Director & Founder of VLChilds/UICF LLC, and the published author of "**Splintered,"** ***Brokenness in the Political Arena.*** **Are We Sacrificing America for Political Gain?** The book, **"Splintered**," **is a** collection of thoughts and experiences from a vast array of everyday people who just want to make America better.

Vivian is a former Congressional Candidate and Congressional District Chairman. Vivian brings passion and energy to serving those in her local community and is noted for performing random acts of kindness. She hosts the "It's Time" Unity Conference which honors outstanding women in different career fields.

Vivian was a Delegate Surrogate at the 2012 Republican National Convention, delivering the first motion from the floor, an alternate delegate to the 2016 RNC convention, and a speaker at the National Women Political Caucus. She champions and hosts a 9/11 ceremony.

Reflections

After writing the poem,

"I Am An American"

many years ago, and reciting it to many across the country, I have decided to put the poem in book form. I have used verse and illustrations to express my heartfelt feeling.

There are pages, at the end of the poem, for you to do the same. The pages are called

"Your Reflections."

Enjoy!

I

am

an

American~

The Constitution

is my source of

strength

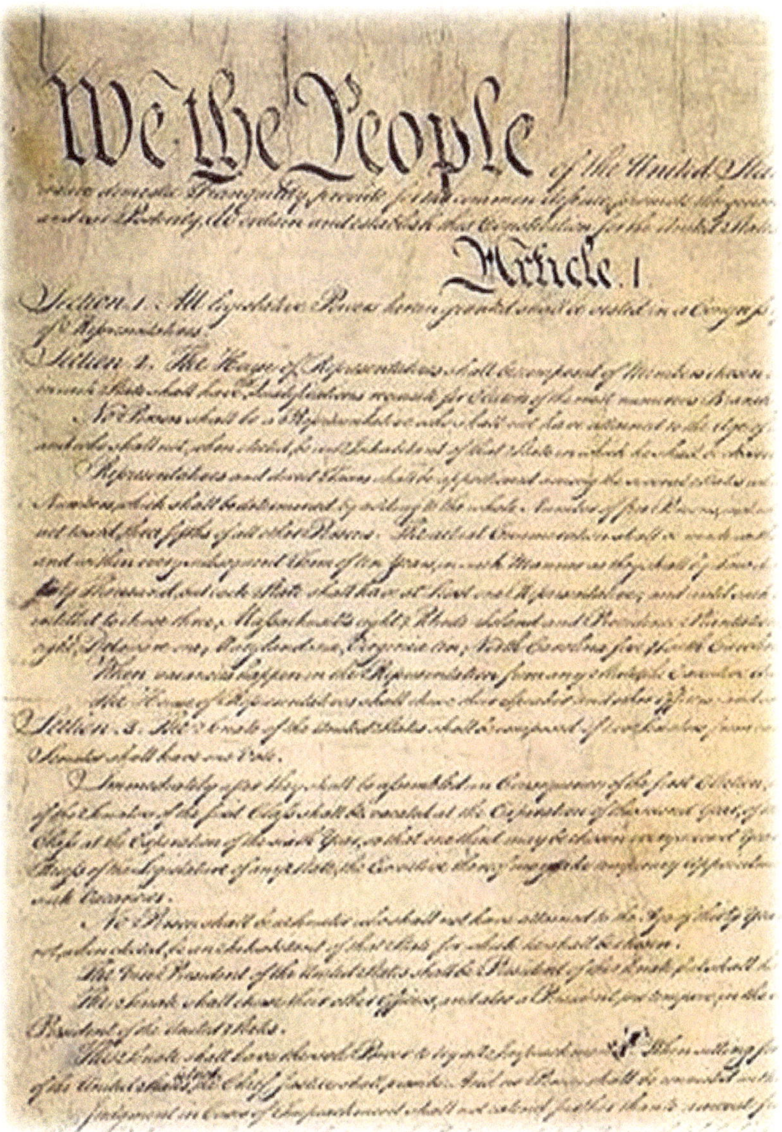

We the People of the United Sta

Article. I

It has **equipped** us with the words necessary to **lead** and **guide** this country.

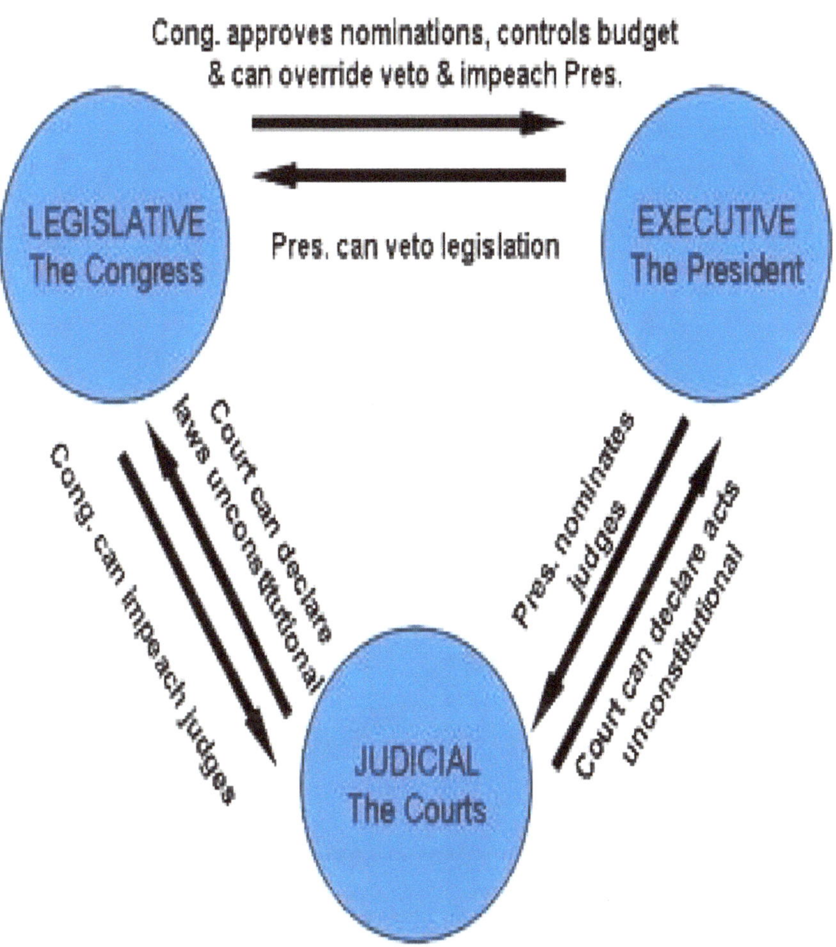
Cong. approves nominations, controls budget
& can override veto & impeach Pres.
Pres. can veto legislation
LEGISLATIVE
The Congress
EXECUTIVE
The President
Court can declare
laws unconstitutional
Cong. can impeach judges
Pres. nominates
judges
Court can declare acts
unconstitutional
JUDICIAL
The Courts

I

am

an

American~

We the
People~

.

I was **born**

in this

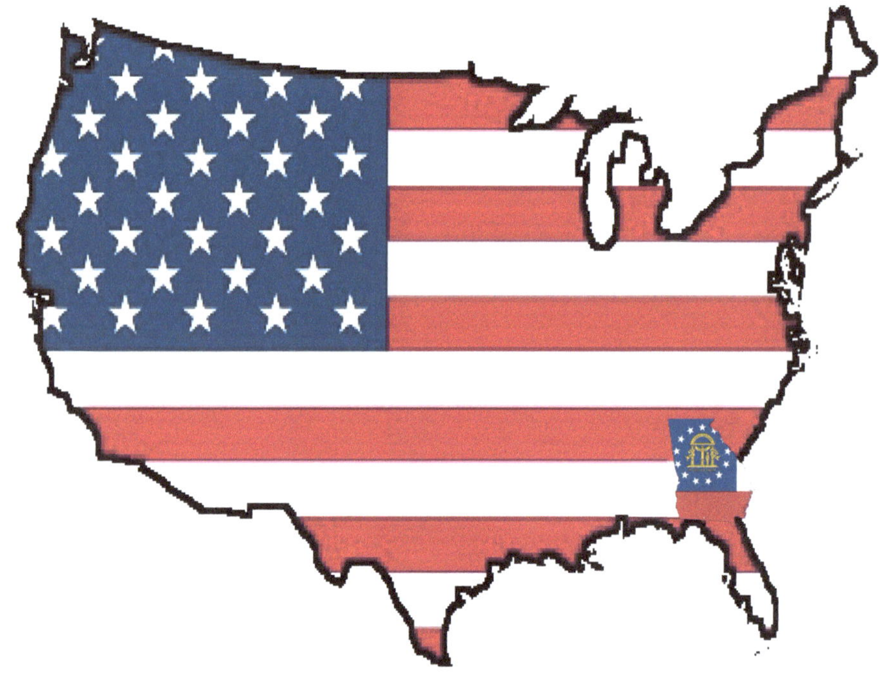

great

country,

CONSTITUTION
WIS
DOM
JUSTICE
MODER
ATION
IN GOD WE TRUST

raised by

parents

who loved me,

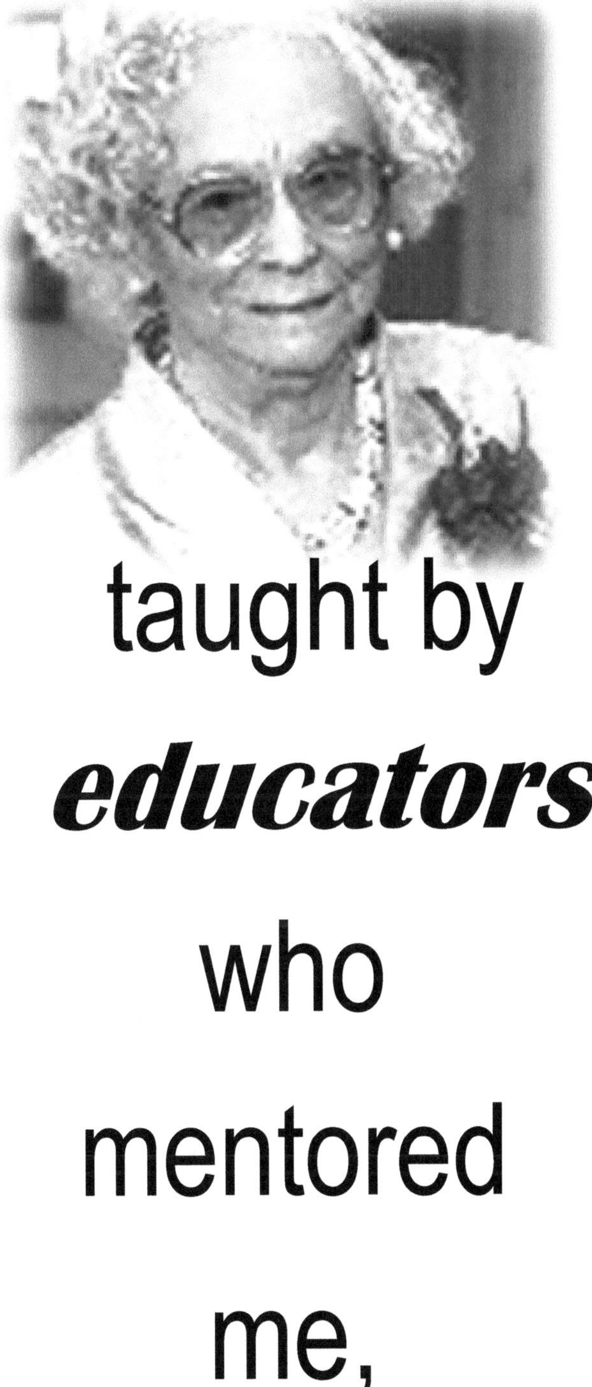

taught by

educators

who

mentored

me,

and

protected

by the

forces

who

defended

me.

I am ***not***

a visitor of

this **land**,

and I am

here

to lend

a hand;

because

I

am,

an

American~

I will

salute

my

country's

flag,

honor

the

men and women

who protect

it, and

pledge

allegiance for

which it

stands.

I will ***not***

apologize for doing

what's right,

be put aside without

a fight,

be sat down,

be tossed around,

or

be shut down.

I will be what

He wants me to be;

patient, determined,

stead***fast***,

and

unmovable

Whatever I am to

an

American~

I know that with hard work and **determination,** this country can be what

our **forefather's** planned it to be.

America,

you can count on me;

because I am,

an

American~

Proud to wear

your colors:

the

Red,

the

White,

the **Blue.**

I am not

ashamed of your

accomplishments,

or

of your

missteps.

I am a **proud**

woman

who is

energized to do

His will.

I only need to

search my heart, ***praise*** the Lord, and ***preach*** His word;

because I ***am,***

an

American~

So ***America***,

please, please ,please

don't give me your

leftovers,

for In the words of a
famous singer,
"I don't want
nobody to give me
nothing,

just open up the
doors and I'll
get it myself."

I am *strong*.

I can't *lose* if **God** is

my focus,

I can't *lose* if

God is my **shield,**

and I can't *lose* if I

trust in

His Word.

You see, I can do

all things

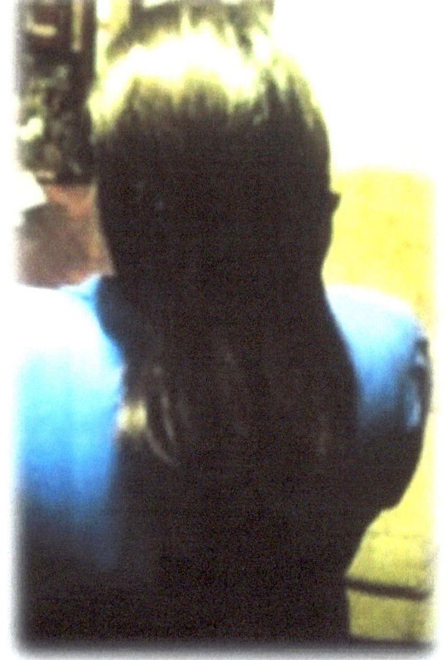

through **Christ**

who

strengthens

me.

This **world** can't

deny me,

burdens can't

weaken me,

sorrow can't slow

me,

disease can't

discourage me,

man can't entice me,

and lust for **fame**

does not own me.

because,

because,

I am

an

American~

Your Reflections~

Your Reflections~

Your Reflections~

Your Reflections~

Your Reflections~

The American dream is only but a dream...until we make it America's reality.

www.ingramcontent.com/pod-product-compliance
Lightning Source LLC
LaVergne TN
LVHW010025070426
835509LV00001B/18

* 9 7 8 0 9 7 9 9 8 9 6 5 0 *